IMAGES OF ENGLAND

HARWICH AND DOVERCOURT
VOLUME II

THE CHRISTENING

THE NEW STEEL STEAMER FOR THE HARWICH ROUTE

THE LUNCHEON

HARWICH

THE "ADELAIDE"

THE BARROW STEEL YARDS

J. TEMPLE

IMAGES OF ENGLAND

HARWICH AND DOVERCOURT
VOLUME II

JOHN MOWLE

TEMPUS

Frontispiece: This print, dated 22 May 1880, tells the story of the
building and launch of the *Adelaide*, the new steel steamer for the
Harwich route to the Hook of Holland. Top left shows the
christening, top right the luncheon and, below, the *Adelaide*
steaming off Harwich. At the bottom are the steel yards that
provided the materials to manufacture the vessel.

First published 2003

Tempus Publishing Limited
The Mill, Brimscombe Port,
Stroud, Gloucestershire, GL5 2QG

© John Mowle, 2003

The right of John Mowle to be identified as the Author of this work has
been asserted in accordance with the Copyrights, Designs and Patents Act
1988.

British Library Cataloguing in Publication Data.
A catalogue record for this book is available from the British Library.

ISBN 0 7524 3084 X

Typesetting and origination by Tempus Publishing Limited
Printed in Great Britain by Midway Colour Print, Wiltshire

Contents

HARWICH & DOVERCOURT CELEBRITIES AS SEEN BY "MATT"

Sunday Graphic of Sunday 31 January 1932, featuring Harwich and Dovercourt celebrities as seen by 'Matt', the paper's resident cartoonist. The likenesses were very good, from the 'dapper' Deputy Mayor, Cllr Ward, to the two local fishermen F. Bowling and Ike Hart.

Introduction

Much has been recorded in terms of pictures of Harwich and Dovercourt, so when I was asked to produce a follow-up to my first book I realised it would be a challenge. As Harwich covers an area of less than three square miles, new material is somewhat difficult to find. However in this edition I have endeavoured to provide previously unpublished material and cover a wider area, including Upper Dovercourt, Tollgate and snapshots of Michaelstowe Hall, Ramsey, Parkeston, Mistley and the Oakleys, together with some interesting aerial photographs.

Upper Dovercourt and Tollgate date back over 1,000 years and were mentioned in the Domesday survey initiated by William I in 1087. At that time twenty-four families lived here under the Lordship of Aubrey de Vere. Dovercourt was an extension of this old village which, with Harwich, was incorporated into a charter granted to the borough by Edward II in 1318. Later James I granted a more ample charter.

Ramsey, it is claimed, possibly pre-dates AD 800, and interesting stories with links to the village are plentiful. It is claimed, for example, that in 1701 the skeleton of one of Claudius's elephants was found buried in Wrabness woods, and if true it could indicate some Roman occupation of this area. Sir Richard Whittington, Lord Mayor of London, is also remembered as one legendary visitor to Ramsey in 1397. Another tale concerns the Lordships of Ray, Wix Abbey, Stoudland, Harwich, Michaelstowe, East Hall and Wrabness, which all came under the Manor of Ramsey. Recently, all these manors were put up for sale with prices between £8,000-£10,000, and I understand that none reached the reserve price.

Michaelstowe took its name from the parish church of St Michael, originally part of the Manor of Ramsey, and was mentioned in the Domesday book. Michaelstowe's separation from Ramsey took place in 1379 when Richard III granted it to Walter Legat and two associates, who then passed it on to the Lordship of St Osyth. Subsequently the Garland family came into possession of all the manors in the mid-1600s.

Parkeston is a comparatively young village earlier called 'Le Rey' and belonging to the Manor of Ramsey. The area was almost all marsh or farmland until Squire Lewis Peake Garland came up with an ambitious scheme in the mid-nineteenth century to dig dykes and drain the marsh, providing him with 1,600 acres of useful land. This development was well timed, as in 1874 the Great Eastern Railway presented plans to develop some deep-water berths and fortunately the squire owned most of the land required. After acquiring the land the GER began the construction of the quay began in 1878. Charles H. Parkes opened the development on 15 February 1883, when the village became known as Parkeston. The GER then decided to build affordable housing for its employees and so Parkeston village was born.

Mistley came to prominence with the arrival of wealthy Richard Rigby in 1703, when he built Mistley Hall, thirty good houses, granaries, warehouses, quays, coal yards and a large malting office. Robert Adam, the famous architect, later improved the village, though Mistley still retains its 'old world charm'.

Lastly we come to the Oakleys. There is evidence dating from the Neolithic period to suggest early occupation of these villages. During the 1950s Dick Farrands, a local archaeologist, discovered the remains of the foundations of a Roman villa, and several more discoveries in fields between the Oakleys point to a fairly large Roman presence. The name Oakley is thought to have come from the Saxon word *Akley*, which means 'plain of woods'. In Saxon times oaks were plentiful and many were felled and used at Harwich for shipbuilding.

New steam lifeboat *Duke of Northumberland* with hydraulic propulsion, 1890. The lifeboat was 50ft long, 14ft wide and, with coal, crew and thirty passengers, had a draught of over 3ft 3in. At the time the boat was very high-tech, constructed of top-quality steel and there were no less than 72,000 rivets used in the hull construction. The boat was driven by a 170hp steam turbine, which delivered water through the outlets at the rate of 1 ton per second, giving a speed of 8 ½ knots; she had a displacement weight of 20 tons. The boat was also fitted with a large lugsail and jib, built by R. & H. Green of Blackwall, and she was on station at Harwich until 1892, being replaced by the *City of Glasgow*.

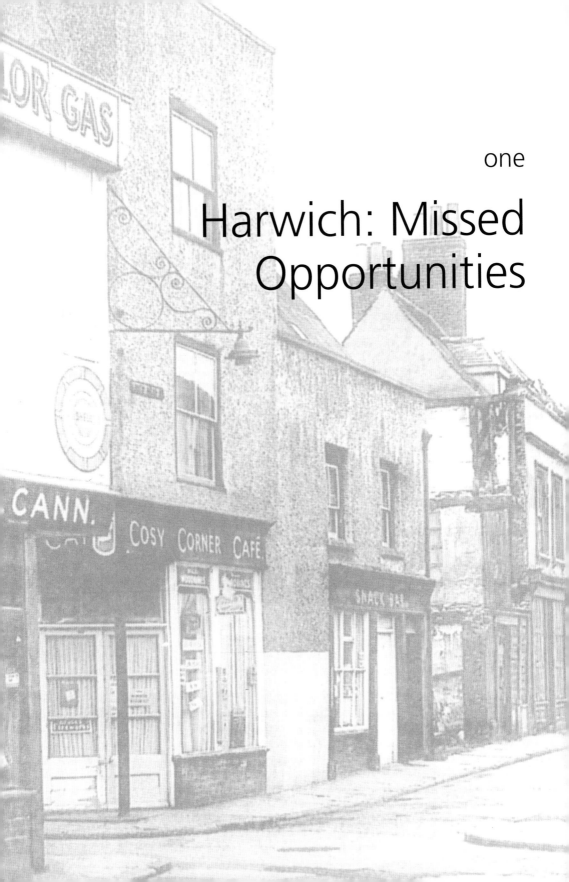

one

Harwich: Missed Opportunities

A winter scene: Kings Quay Street, early 1950s. The building on the left was Self's hardware shop and is now the Bear restaurant. Next to this was J. Barker's homemade sweets' shop, then Middleton's ships' chandlers, Don's Café, Neal's fruit and veg shop and lastly Fred Watling's corner shop. Don's Café had a rather dubious reputation as a meeting place for the lads after the pubs 'chucked out' at night. Fry-ups were always available there through to the early hours. Apart from the Bear, the remainder of the properties have long since been converted into living accommodation.

The Spread Eagle (previously known as the Star), West Street, 1951. A public house has been on this site since 1680. Harwich lost much of its drinking trade during the late 1960s and '70s due mainly to the closure of the Reserve fleet and the Transit Camp. This pub was not alone in finding a living hard to make and was eventually sold and converted into flats. The Fountain Fisheries next door has been renamed Piseas and still sells quality 'Harwich' fish and chips.

Above left: Currents Lane *c*.1960. The British Flag on the right was owned by Claude and Lydia Whitnal. This lane was home to a multitude of shops on both sides. They included Denny's fish shop, Wasserman's boot shop, Sach fruiterers, Bentliff hardware, British and Argentine Meat Company and many more specialist shops. These picturesque narrow streets were one of the more appealing sights in old Harwich until the Council decided to demolish not only all the left-hand side of Currents Lane but also great chunks of West Street and Church Street to make way for a modern block of flats. Despite this, the designers of the new buildings, which bear no resemblance to the demolished properties, won an award.

Above right: St Austin's Lane, *c*.1956. Another lovely narrow street full of shops. On the right at the end stands the Half Moon public house, soon to be closed and used as an antiques shop. All the left-hand side was demolished to make way for the much maligned area No.1, a new flats development and 'another nail in the coffin'.

Left: Esplanade School in the 1950s. The school dated back to the early 1800s and was very basic with few amenities. The building underwent rebuilding in the 1850s, but suffered considerable damage during the 1953 flood and finally closed in 1960. It was later used for several commercial purposes, such as the depot for Baum & Watts (who used to supply the pirate radio ship *Caroline*), and the Wellington slipper company. The building was later demolished and replaced with a modern block of flats.

Two views of Kings Head Street, *c.*1950. The upper view shows the derelict state of these properties at that time, and also shows the very attractive shopfronts of the Georgian period built on to a much earlier construction. In the 1900s the street formed part of a bustling prosperous town. Unfortunately the advent of the rail link, the departure of 'the fleet' based at the harbour and the development of more modern shops at nearby Dovercourt caused Harwich to fall into decline. The local council chose the trendy option to demolish these buildings and replace them with blocks of flats. The development was named area No.2. This followed area No.1, which controversially included the demolition of a great number of historic shop and house buildings in Market Street, Wellington Road, Kings Head Street and St Austin's Lane.

The picture on the right shows Cosy Corner Café and the long-established Canns chandlers shop. Cosy Corner Café had a very colourful history. It had been a grocers, art gallery, antique shop and, soon after this photograph was taken, it became the venue for the recently formed Harwich Boxing Club run by Peter Brooks, a local businessman. Canns was converted to a private residence and the Cosy Corner Café is currently also being converted to residential use.

Above: Apricity, the last coal coaster to unload at Gashouse Creek, 1965. This vessel made regular trips to Harwich laden with coal, the raw material for the town's gas. By-products of gas manufacture provided the town with tar, creosote and coke. The coke was used mainly in commercial boilers, but, being less expensive than coal, would also be used as fuel in the home. The creek was used by the fishing community as well, and several fishing boats can be seen in the picture.

Left: The Gas Works, *c*.1965. At this time the buildings were being demolished and the site cleared, as the advent of North Sea gas had rendered the works obsolete; Harwich therefore lost its cheap source of fuel. Since then the site has mainly been unused and the creek has silted up, now awaiting its fate.

The Palace Cinema engine room in 1969, showing the huge Crossley gas engine used to drive the generator to produce the electricity needed to run the cinema. The engine, driven by gas, was manufactured in 1899 and weighed almost 3½ tons. Having a massive flywheel of 7ft diameter, it only revved at 180rpm. An ex-Crossley engineer inspected the engine in 1975 and declared it as beyond repair. This decision was made too hastily, as several missing parts were still in the locality. Also, Budworths, the local engineering firm, had expressed an interest in making replica parts. At that time the engine could have been removed via the empty plot next to the Palace. The remains sadly lay below ground level in the abandoned engine room!

Barrack Lane, c.1900. This very early photograph shows the lane before any housing had been built and it was the main road to the Redoubt fort. The tents of the Redoubt troops can be seen on barrack field.

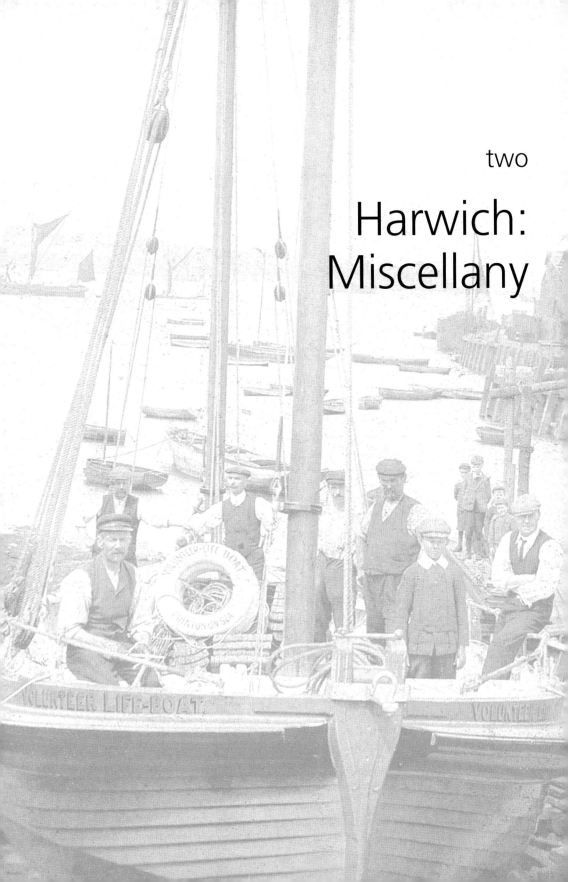

two

Harwich: Miscellany

Prince George visited Harwich on 24 April 1924. The picture shows Prince George with Commissioner Mrs Gladys Gooch inspecting the Harwich District Girl Guides after inaugurating the Harwich-Zeebrugge train ferry service. He then inspected the Brownies before boarding a steamer for Felixstowe.

MV *Stella Polaris* at Harwich, *c.*1952. This elegant ship was launched on 11 September 1926 and joined the Bergen Line of Norway. Built with luxury cruising in mind, the passengers were mainly Americans. The ship would sail out of New York for a round-the-world voyage finishing up at Harwich. In 1948 she also brought visitors to London for the Olympic Games. Seized by the Germans during the Second World War, the *Stella Polaris* was used as a floating recreation centre for submarine officers. After the war the ship was handed back to the owners where she underwent an expensive overhaul and in 1951 was sold to the Clipper Line. The *Stella Polaris* continued cruising until 1969 when she was sold to a Japanese company for use as a floating hotel. The ship remains at Kisho Nishira in Japan and is still a tourist attraction.

An 1885 print depicting some of the more interesting views of old Harwich. Top left is the Halfpenny Pier, top right the Parade, and centre left is Market Street viewed from Kings Quay Street. Centre right is a view of the old slipway on Jetty Shore and the High Lighthouse. The bottom two pictures show the beach and a lovely view of the busy quayside.

Above: Smith's Greengrocers situated at 21 Market Street, *c.*1925. Fortunately the shopfront remains in almost original condition. Behind the shop there is a beautiful carving that has become known as the 'Little Queen of Market Street'. Further back into the rear of the building there is another carving of a 'King'. Historians came to the conclusion that these carvings were originally part of a much earlier building, which could have been the large Elizabethan mansion believed to have once occupied this site.

Right: Swan Stores in 1921. Previously a public house, it had been known as The Ship, The Crown, the Bell and Dragon, and finally The Swan. After the First World War the last landlord, George Cooper, converted the right-hand side of the pub into a general store aptly named Swan Stores. This fifteenth-century building fell into decline in the 1960s and was later purchased, restored and converted into private accommodation.

Bernard & Sons tailors shop, Church Street, 1932. The shop was owned by T.H. Bernard, outfitters to the Royal Navy, who owned a factory a short distance away in Main Road. The firm made uniforms for most of the departments of the armed forces. The photograph shows a staff muster outside the shop. The large number of staff were definitely needed as they made bespoke high-quality clothing at the time. Pictured, left to right, are George Poole, Mr Taylor, Lillian ?, ? Farrow, Alf Bury (Manager), –?–, –?–, –?–.

Daniel Hogg's general store situated in Talbot Street, Bathside, *c*.1920. Pictured left to right are Daniel's daughter, Daniel Hogg and Daniel's wife Violet.

The Angel public house on the Quay, 1950s. This quayside pub was a popular meeting place for naval officers from the reserve fleet moored in the river as well as those from HMS *Ganges*; the Army was also represented, with staff from HQ Movement Control at the Transit Camp at Tollgate. Parked outside is a Rolls Royce model 20/25 owned by the licensee, Major (Ken) Kendal. The Angel was built in 1824 and the lease taken by Thomas Cobbold, the local brewer. Harwich Borough Council once owned the building, which was sold in 1999 to the Milsom Group and restored as an annexe to the Pier Hotel.

An Ike Hart discovery, 1964. Whilst carrying out repairs to the kerbstones in Kings Head Street, Ike came across an underground structure. After close examination it was established that it was a 'rain back', well-built underground rainwater storage compartments. Harwich has many of these rain backs, with most of the older houses sometimes having two or three.

Right: A thank you card from Mr Rounds, 1886. Mr Rounds was the successful parliamentary candidate for Harwich and personal thank you cards seemed to be the order of the day. How nice it would be if that practice were followed today!

Below: Dornier flying boat N25, March 1927. The flying boat was on a trial flight from Horten in Norway to Harwich to test the viability of an Anglo-Norwegian airmail service. Amongst the mail was a letter from King Haakon of Norway to King George V. The pilot of the flying boat was Lt Luetzow Holm, and Roald Amundsen had previously used this aircraft for his North Pole expedition in 1925. Three trial mail flights were made but after evaluation it was decided that the mail service would prove too expensive.

HARWICH

OR

NORTH EAST ESSEX ELECTION

JULY 16th, 1886.

ROUND	-	-	4623
WICKS -	-	-	2322
Majority		-	2301

With Mr. Round's Compliments and THANKS.

Left: The Frinton volunteer lifeboat at Harwich, 1907. Named *The Sailors Friend*, she was a pulling and sailing lifeboat of the Suffolk and Norfolk type said to be designed by David Cook, an old Lowestoft beach man who moved to Frinton in about 1900. The lifeboat was built by J&H Cann of Harwich and was launched on 5 August 1907; she was christened with a bottle of seawater, as the crew were all teetotallers. The lifeboat led an eventful life with many heroic rescues to her credit and went off station in 1917.

Right: Arthur and Kate Butler with their children on a cold day on the Esplanade, *c.*1928. The church of St Nicholas with its associated buildings is visible in the background.

Opposite page, below: Charabanc outside The New Bell, *c.*1928, with regulars seated ready to depart on their outing with wives and children in attendance. Outside the charabanc, from left to right, are Dorothy Smith, Sam Smith, Mabel Smith, Mabel Ada Smith and Jack (Nig) Smith. At the front is Joe Smith jnr. Behind the screen, with cap and moustache, is Joe Smith snr. The building to the left of the New Bell is the Soup Kitchen, where a bowl of soup cost 1d if you could afford it and was free if you couldn't.

Above: David Wills' baker's shop dressed up for Empire Day celebrations, *c.*1930. The shop was situated in Church Street between Blosse tobacconist and the drapery shop owned by Mr Austin. Great efforts were made to use only Empire-made ingredients in goods for sale. In the shop window on the left a display of Easter eggs can clearly be seen. There was also a small tearoom between the shop and bakery, which was situated at the rear in Kings Head Street. David also owned a shop at Tollgate aptly named 'The Cake Shop', which was run by his sister Florence.

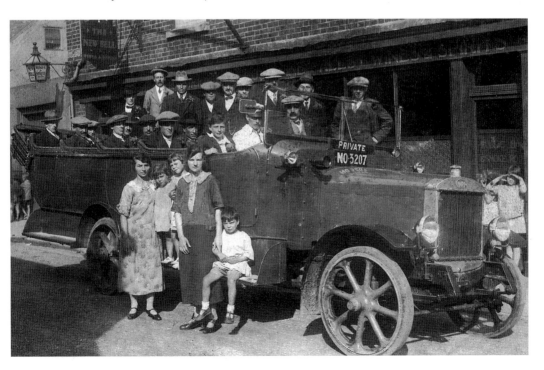

The Co-op Grocery Store at 20 Church Street, *c*.1880. The Co-op opened its first shop in Harwich in 1874 at 20 Market Street then transferred to 20 Church Street in 1887. The Co-op was formed in Rochdale, Lancashire in 1844 with the object of providing its members and the general public with groceries, drapery, boots, shoes, bread, butcher's meat, milk, coal etc. It also aimed to seek the domestic, social and intellectual advancement of its members. After serving the Harwich community for over 125 years, the shop was closed in 1999.

Harwich Green, August 1953. So many families were left homeless in the aftermath of the East Coast flood that the council had to provide temporary accommodation for the victims. Harwich Green was chosen for this purpose and over 100 caravans with adjoining sheds were sited there. Water standpipes were put in place and paths laid. The Green became a small community within Harwich, and the more unfortunate families were forced to endure conditions on this site for over two years.

three

Upper
Dovercourt

Left above: The Bungalow, *c.*1928. This was the home of Joseph Gant, hurdlemaker, who carried out his trade at the rear of the property. Piles of hurdles were to be seen stacked to some 12ft high at times .The Bungalow stood between Pound Farm and Nightingale's bakery and shop. After demolition in 1956 a large car showroom was built on the site for S.W. Crawley whose garage was opposite.

THE COTTAGE HOSPITAL, DOVERCOURT BAY.

Above: The Monks Houses, *c.*1900 (opposite All Saints Church). These houses were granted to the Monks of Coln in a charter from Roger Bigod, Earl of Norfolk, together with the church and all things belonging to it. Upon the dissolution of the Priory of Coln in 1536, the ownership reverted to King Henry VIII. Pictured on the right is the wheelwrights belonging to Ethan Cutting, and to the left of the cottages is the blacksmiths of Edgar Cutting.

Opposite middle: The Grange, *c.*1930. This elegant house was built in 1911 for the Hepworth family and included every modern labour-saving device. The 7-acre estate also had a lodge house and a large double garage with chauffeur's room. The gardens were beautifully landscaped with formal gardens, large ponds, an orchard and kitchen garden together with many specimen trees. During the First World War the house and grounds were requisitioned and used by the military as a convalescent home. When peacetime arrived The Grange was bought by the Misses Lilley who carried out further landscaping and approached Liberties of London to update the interior. In 1939, fearing that the proposed Warner's Holiday Lido would interfere with their unobstructed sea views, the sisters sold the house and grounds to Essex County Council. It was later to become a centre for further education and is presently used as a sixth-form college.

Opposite below: The Harwich and District Hospital and Fryatt Memorial, 1939. Previously a private house (Rosebank) this property was purchased with donations including £2,100 from GER, which was part of the salvage money from the SS *Brussels* in memory of her captain, Charles Fryatt. The hospital opened in 1922 and the 1939 annual report shows that 391 patients were admitted to the hospital during that year, including a large number of casualties from the Dutch liner *Simon Bolivar* which was mined off Harwich. Some other notable donations were also received, including £25 from the Harwich Guy Carnival, £10 from the Harwich Charity Cup and a legacy or £2,000 from R.C. Abdy esq; the total salaries for 1939 were a meagre £1,051 3s 11d. The hospital is now under threat of closure to provide a site for a more modern compact hospital and health centre.

Left: King George VI visited All Saints Church on 11 July 1940. The king was on a visit to the area to inspect the coastal defences.

Above: Butchers shop of A.P. Lilley, *c.*1935. Known as 'West End Butchers', it was situated on Main Road between Keeling's fish shop and Colin's grocery store. Mr Lilley started his butchery business at the turn of the century and continued trading until the early 1950s, when the shop was sold to the Co-op.

Opposite below: Crawley's Garage 1926. Pictured left to right are Mrs Crawley, Percy Howlett (trainee), Mr Crawley and an unknown customer. As the early motorcar was very unreliable and prone to breakdown, Mr Crawley's engineering skills proved useful. Spares were scarce at the time and he would manufacture or repair these himself, hence gaining his garage a good reputation.

Above: The Crawley Bros' Agrimotor, 1913. In 1912, at the age of fourteen, Samuel Crawley made a prototype motor plough that could also be converted into a tractor. With the help of his brother it went into production in 1913. Over seventy of these ploughs were made and sold worldwide. The 18ft-long machine was powered by an American Buda engine producing 30bhp. The introduction of the Fordson tractor priced the Agrimotor out of the market and in 1925 the Crawley brothers sold their Saffron Waldon works, Samuel Crawley moving to Upper Dovercourt to start a garage business there.

Crawley's Garage, 1954. Soon to outgrow the original building, Mr Crawley built a new front part to include an office and small showroom in 1928. The garage later became main agents for BSA motorcycles and the leading Austin/Morris agents for the area. The garage provided jobs for five skilled mechanics, four apprentices and one office worker. The garage was renowned for its high-quality workmanship and old-fashioned niceties. On Mr Crawley's retirement the business was sold, but was never able to recapture its former reputation. It was eventually demolished and retirement homes now occupy this site.

Upper Dovercourt War Memorial, c.1926. The Memorial was unveiled in 1920 to commemorate the loss of life during the First World War. On the left of the picture are Colin's grocery store and post office, A.P. Lilley butchers, Bert Keeling fishmonger, Crawley's Garage, the Cabin restaurant, Nightingale fruiterer and confectioner, and finally the Church of England infants' school.

The Hill School lower seven football team of 1949. From left to right, back row: Dennis Rowland, Brian Tovell, Malcolm Tye, Ralph Smith, Frank Freestone, Mick Fletcher and Ron Feaviour. Front row: Eric Honeycombe, Fred Frostick, George Newbury, George Ricketts, Mike Hazelton, Barry Smith, Mick Chester and Mick Shears. There is no report of any of these players making the Premier League!

The Trafalgar Quoits team of the 1920s, proudly showing off their trophies and medals attached to their watch chains. One wonders if the wearing of large flat caps guarantees success in the game of quoits!

Girls' Training Corps, 1947. The band on parade on their way to the church. From left to right: bass drum Beryl Moles, ? Tye, Marge Ling, Cynthia Parkin, Ann Oxborrow, Pat Humphrey and Beryl Tye. The Commandant was Mrs Graystone.

Main Road Musical and Electrical Stores, c.1930. Frank Petch at his Upper Dovercourt shop, premises also existing at 63 High Street, Dovercourt. The shop sold radios and electrical goods and, as well as being an authorised Columbia record dealer, it also boasted carrying the largest stock of gramophones in the district. The shop is now the Upper Dovercourt post office.

Gathering of the Hunt, May 1927. Upper Dovercourt Green provided a regular venue for the gathering of the Essex and Suffolk foxhounds. This event would always bring out a large crowd of onlookers and hunt followers. There were of course many more acres of open farmland at that time.

Tea party on Upper Dovercourt Green, 1945. VE day was celebrated up and down the country and Upper Dovercourt was no exception. Trestle tables were erected, ration coupons pooled and refreshments provided to celebrate the British forces' victory in Europe.

Above: Ainger's Sawmill bungalow, Main Road, *c.*1920. The bungalow, built by the Ainger family, was first made in sections on the Green then transported across the road to a site adjoining the sawmills and reassembled. The Ainger sawmills provided the prepared wood for many local projects, including the All Saints Church lych-gate, the Frinton lifeboat and barges built by Canns of Harwich. Pictured outside are, left to right, Jimmy, Jack, Ted and Harry Ainger.

Left: Billy Last, shoemaker, with his child outside his premises on the Green, *c.*1880. As well as making bespoke boots and shoes, Billy's second job was that of village postman, as his uniform would suggest.

four

Tollgate

Above: John Flatt with his milk float, Tollgate Farm, *c.*1947. John was the grandson of the farm manager, James Flatt. By this time the Co-op had hired three more farms, High House Farm, Vicarage Farm and Burnt House Farm at Ramsey. They also hired another 13 acres of land from Ramsey Lodge. These farms enabled them to vastly increase milk production, and at this time there were four milk floats carrying out milk deliveries daily.

Tollgate corner viewed from the west, showing Tollgate Farmhouse, *c*.1910. This farmhouse, along with all the surrounding land, was owned by Robert Bagshaw. The farm itself was leased to the Co-operative Society as part of its dairy enterprise, and was managed by Mr Flatt, the farm bailiff.

Right: A map of Tollgate Farm, with 5 acres of land, 1876. The field on the left was known as Trafalgar Field. This, together with the larger field to the right, were purchased for the Council housing development of Abdy Avenue in 1927, and named after the High Steward of Harwich, Richard Coombe Abdy. The bottom field was later to become an extension to Abdy Avenue in the 1950s. The plot top right was sold in 1925 and developed in 1932 when two houses and four shops were built here.

Opposite below: Tollgate corner viewed from the east, *c*.1910. This charming picture shows a caravan on the land that was later to become the site for a new public house, the Devonshire Arms. The narrow road left, to Oakley, and the open landscape with established trees, indicates just how rural Tollgate was at this time.

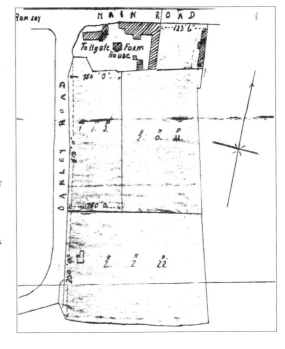

Haymaking at Tollgate Farm, 1890. The group of farm labourers take a well-earned rest. James Flatt, the farm bailiff, is pictured on the left.

The Sparrow family and other employees at work at Tollgate Farm, August 1914. George Sparrow is centre.

High House Farm, Tollgate, *c.*1916. The grooms of the Essex Regiment pose with the regiment's horses, which were stabled at the farm. The soldiers were tented in a field directly opposite the farm, although the main body of the regiment was billeted at the Redoubt.

Gypsy caravan, Southhall Farm, Oakley Road, Tollgate, *c.*1930. The caravan was sited near the farm pond. The owner Mr Shellock was employed by the farm owner, Mr Creswell, as a labourer. Mr Shellock stayed working on the farm until his death in the late 1940s, and the caravan was given the traditional gypsy send off when it was set alight with all its contents.

Main Road Garage Tollgate, *c*.1950. This garage was previously a barn belonging to Tollgate Farm but Mr Rogers converted it and carried on his business there until the outbreak of the Second World War. The building was taken over by the military, which used it to store and maintain Bren-gun carriers for the Czech Armoured Regiment stationed locally. After the war the garage was purchased by Mr George Dawdry, who moved his workshop from its location near the Green. Mr Dawdry continued trading until the 1960s. Pictured outside the garage is Mr Bob Fosker on his Brough Superior motorcycle combination.

Tollgate Cottage, *c.*1900, owned by Robert Bagshaw with tenant Mrs Johnson outside. It has been suggested that the Tollgate turnpike was possibly situated opposite Vicarage Farm. However there is strong evidence to indicate that the Tollgate was close to Tollgate Cottage, which was nearer to the junction with Oakley Road.

Above: Dove House Farmhouse, *c.*1950. The farmhouse was part of the 73-acre Dove House estate, stretching from Tollgate to Gypsy Lane and across from Oakley Road to Ramsey Road. In 1934 the estate was divided into plots and sold by the Smith family for building land. The farmhouse and a small parcel of land was retained by the Smiths and rented to Mr Taylor for use as a smallholding. The picture shows Mrs Taylor with her granddaughter, Margaret.

Left: The Dovecote, Dove House Farm, *c.*1948. Mr Taylor and his son Ted are pictured beside the magnificent dovecote.

Opposite above: A game shoot, Smythies Farm, 1914. There were thirteen farms within the parish of Dovercourt at this time providing a plentiful supply of pheasants, partridges, rabbits and hares. The farmers and sportsmen are gathered after enjoying a day's shooting. Alf Gant, the farm owner, is pictured third from left.

Ramsey Lodge garden, 1943. During 1943 members of the Czech Independent Armoured Division were stationed in Dovercourt. Their headquarters were at Ramsey Lodge and many of the troops were billeted with local families. Tollgate children were made very welcome at the Lodge and the picture shows a group at one of the parties laid on by the soldiers. From left to right, front row: Wreford Tibbenam, Barbara Howlett, Peter Clover, Arthur Clover, Dave Poole, Brian Leeks, Doug Morsley, Doug Griggs, Stan Howlett, Colin Gowers. Second row: Maureen Howlett, Greta Morsley, Doreen Dean, Irene Frostick, Marjorie Morsley, Rita Leeks, Sheila Smith, Czech Soldier, Brian Campbell. Back row: Czech officer and three cooks.

Tollgate United football team, 1949. After the Second World War the Tollgate menfolk were anxious to return to normality and the war veterans decided to set up a football club. It soon became apparent that to be successful, some younger blood would have to be recruited. From left to right, front row: Stan Howlett, Len Eagle, Ray Leeks, Don Simpson, ? Goff, Doug Morsley. Back row: Tommy Sands, -?-, -?-, Jack Leeks, -?-, -?-, Titch Double, Vivien Pilbeam, Jim Tilley.

Tollgate United Women's *v* Men's Challenge match, 1949. Here we have the Tollgate women's scratch team lined up against the men for a fun event. From left to right, front row: Don Simpson, Bill Goldsmith, Stan Howlett, Ellie Double, Titch Double, Terry Honnybell. Back row: Whinny Simpson, Eileen Howlett, Mrs Harris, Eileen Smith, Bunty Harris, Beryl Knappet, Eddy Smith and Les Raybold in drag.

Above: Tollgate 'scruffs', Summer 1949. The Devonshire Arms pub had a very large car park, which became a meeting point and playground for the young Tollgate children. This photograph captures some of the youngsters. From left to right, front row: Janice Smith, Bill Dean, Val Dean and Fred Scutcher. Back row: Margaret Smith, Peter Atkins, Peter Smith, Bob Dean, Sheila Smith, Leslie Smith and Maureen Howlett.

Left: The Transit Camp, 1956. This large camp was built by German prisoners of war towards the end of the Second World War, for the use of military personnel returning to England from the Continent. Pictured is a group of Catering Corps staff who made it their business to see that the troops were well fed. Pictured, from left to right, are: -?-, -?-, -?-, -?-, Roy Budd, Keith Prior, John Mead. The camp could house up to 3,000 servicemen and 750 meals could be provided in one sitting.

Above: Tollgate United Social Club dance, All Saints Church Hall, February 1950. From left to right, front row: Maureen Howlett, Brian Campbell, Arthur Clover, Ralph Smith, Cath Simpson, Terry Honybell, Alan Avis, Barry Whitman. Middle row: Mrs Honybell, Barbara Howlett, Greta Morsley, Pat Harris, Marg Lord, Joan Hales, Betty Lacey, Titch Double and John Dean. Back row: Derek Lungley, Les Avis, Mr Harris, -?-, -?-, Jack Howlett, Sheila Race, Alan Hinds, ? Osgood, Dorothy Barker. Band at rear: Mrs Whitman, -?-, Jim Farthing, ? Wickens.

W. Gooch shop and post office, 1954. Mr Gooch purchased the shop from Mr Scott in 1944. Pictured in the doorway is shop assistant Jenny Atkins.

Above: Aerial view of High House Farm, *c.*1959. Don and John Simpson continued running the farm on the retirement of their father, Rodney, in 1947. They built up a successful dairy herd as well as producing arable crops. Sadly the farm was sold for building land and the farm and its buildings no longer exist.

Opposite below: Gooch's shop staff in 1954, caught on camera by a Birds' custard salesman. Pictured are Maureen Lilley and Jenny Atkins with shop manager Christopher Pennick, who took over the running of the shop on the death of Mr Gooch. The shop specialised in home-cooked hams, stationery and hardware, as well as general provisions. The post office was housed in an adjoining building.

VICARAGE FARM
─── DAIRY ───
DOVERCOURT

*All Milk supplied from Tuberculin
Tested Cows and Produced on
Local Farms*

TELEPHONE   HARWICH   15

Please Mention Town Guide

Left: Vicarage Farm delivery van, *c.*1953. Pictured is Wally Southgate, one of the farm's five delivery drivers. The farm was the last to produce, bottle and deliver milk locally.

Below: Soldiers believed to be from the Worcestershire Regiment, Tollgate, 1913. The tents were pitched on the field opposite High House Farm and formed part of the Tollgate garrison which covered the protection of the coast between Dovercourt and Earlham's beach. The houses in the background are those in the picture opposite top.

Road widening at Oakley Road corner, 1921. The main road to Oakley at this time was not much more than a country lane, and with motor transport becoming more common it was felt that on safety grounds it would be prudent to widen this almost right-angled corner.

MR. & MRS. A. E. BYE

HOST AND HOSTESS AT THE

DEVONSHIRE ARMS

UPPER DOVERCOURT

Invite Your Patronage At Dovercourt's Newest Hotel - The Last Word in Modern Comfort - Luxurious Lounge - Musical Evenings - Congenial Company

SNACKS A SPECIALITY

SPACIOUS ACCOMMODATION FOR CARS AND COACHES

Newspaper advert for the new Devonshire Arms Hotel, April 1938.

Devonshire Arms Hotel, *c*.1950, under the management of Harry and Elsie Smith. Messrs Cobbold & Co. had this building erected during 1937/38 and it opened in April 1938 as the most modern hotel in the area. This development included two large bars panelled in oak and the saloon bar had a lift installed to the kitchen where freshly made sandwiches and snacks were prepared. On the first floor there was ample accommodation for the licensee as well as five luxurious guest rooms. Outside, a large area of reinforced concrete provided parking space for 150-200 cars. There was also a York stone-paved garden area and five large, heated lock-up garages. Sadly the trend to 'modernise' has taken away a great deal of the original charm, but it still survives as a public house.

five

Michaelstowe Hall

Members of the Essex and Suffolk Hunt meet at the Hall, November 1911. The imposing Georgian mansion provides the perfect backdrop for the hunt to gather. Chauffeurs watch beside their cars after dropping off the gentry.

Squire Garland and his family pose for a 'Wallis' photograph at the fête in 1913.

The Harwich Church Lads Brigade Band entertains the visitors at the July 1913 fête in Michaelstowe Hall grounds.

Michaelstowe fête, July 1913. Fêtes and garden parties were a frequent feature in life at the Hall and here we have the competitors lined up for the fancy dress and decorated bicycle competition.

Construction of Michaelstowe Hall, 1903. The first recorded date for the Manor of Michaelstowe is
1379. In 1639 the Darvall family became its owners; they also held the Manor of Wrabness. During that
time they established an education facility for the unusual purpose of educating the six oldest men and
the six oldest women of the parish. In 1903 Arthur Garland rebuilt the Manor in grand Georgian style,
with every conceivable luxury including its own electric generator and central heating. It is interesting
to note that the *East Anglian Daily News* reported, on 11 May 1903, that about thirty workmen went on
strike for an extra half pence an hour. Mr Grimwood, the contractor, promptly refused their demands
and paid them off, whereupon they marched round the village singing 'Britons never shall be slaves',

although the greater portion of the workmen resumed work the same day. 1920 saw the estate put up for sale and Mr Richard Coombe Abdy purchased it and moved in. He was a very wealthy man, with business interests in cotton and banking, and had many residences abroad. During Squire Abdy's tenure the grounds were maintained by sixty gardeners and Mr Abdy would offer his guests £1 if they could find a weed anywhere. In 1946 the forty-roomed mansion became Chafford School, an Approved School for boys. Between its aristocratic past and its change to a school the Hall was used as a convalescent home, a military camp and an officers' club. It is now a residential and nursing home for the elderly.

Left: Ramsey Bridge, Autumn 1913. Captain Casement of HMS *Blanche* and one of his senior officers march back to Michaelstowe Hall where his crew are taking part in an exercise. Could the pair have been visiting The Castle or Lord Nelson pub for some light refreshment?

The crew of HMS *Blanche* at Michaelstowe, September 1913. HMS *Blanche*, a Scout Class Cruiser, was launched in 1908; she was moored at Harwich as part of the fleet. The crew had been polishing their signalling skills from the rear of the Hall to the signal tower at HMS *Ganges* across the river at Shotley, under the guidance of the instructors from the Shotley Signal School.

Captain J.M. Casement marches the crew of HMS *Blanche* back to Harwich past the gates of the Hall; SBA Glen Smith (the tall sailor) watches by the gate.

six

Ramsey

Above left: The windmill at Ramsey, *c.*1930. Said to have been moved from Woodbridge in 1842 by Henry Collins, millwright, and erected in Ramsey for Robert Brooks, the windmill remained in their family until 1937. The mill, bakery and cottages were sold by Brooks' executors to Charlotte Coupland who in turn sold the mill to R.M. Scott (biscuit-maker) of Ipswich. In 1939 the sail shutters were removed, and for thirty-five years the windmill was left to the elements. It was sold to private owners in 1974. The mill still stands as a landmark in the village.

Above right: Workmen taking a tea break whilst painting the mill, *c.*1930.

Hill House fire, 1915. Eighteen months after the new owners took over, a serious fire broke out and caused substantial damage. It was the prompt action of the farm workers and local folk who formed a bucket chain that controlled the fire and limited the damage. Pictured are the workers with the local police constable.

Above: Harvest time at Hill House Farm, *c.*1930. Mr Hewitt, on the left, with his farm labourers.

Opposite below: Hill House, 1913. This building was part of a large estate owned by the Hempson family for over 300 years. On the death of Amis Hempson in 1912, the whole estate was divided into eighteen lots of various sizes and sold at auction. Hill House Farm, along with Blanes and Whitehouse Farms, was included in one lot together with 300 acres of land and labourers' cottages. The house and grounds were well appointed with heated conservatory and lean-to vinery, harness room, stables and coach-house with a full-size tennis lawn to the rear. The lot sold for £7,050.

Left: Mrs Maria Lungley outside her cottage during the 1940s.

Below: Street scene, *c.*1905. The residents appear to be posing for the camera outside The Gables.

The Castle Inn, 1912; landlord George Hood. Members of the quoits team are seen preparing to depart in a horse-drawn 'chara' for their annual outing. Amongst the team members are Mr Neal Lungley, Mr Ellis, Mr Farrington, Mr Button and Mr Deex. Standing at the door is Mr Whiting, the local fishmonger, who lived in Cellar Cottages. The village once boasted four public houses.

The Lord Nelson, *c*.1928. This was another of the village pubs, having its own nursery garden and orchard. The Nelson closed in 1961, and is now a private house.

Cellar Cottages, the Street, 1910, so named because the door opened directly to steps leading to the cellar. The lady outside could possibly be Mrs Whiting.

Frank Ellis's yard, *c.*1924. Mr Ellis was a builder, decorator and funeral director. The hearse was horse-drawn, the horse being the same one that pulled the builder's cart. Mr George 'Charlie' Fulcher was one of the employees; Charlie was a bricklayer, grave digger and hearse driver. The fence in the background is that of Pullin, the coal merchant. The yard has since been demolished and redeveloped for housing.

Ramsey Quoits team presentation, 1930s. A proud Bill Pryke receiving his award from Arthur Goddard, with Percy Farrington watching.

The blacksmiths on Church Hill, *c*.1912. In the centre of the picture we can see a cart wheel being trundled out from the blacksmith's yard, the blacksmith being Mr King. Polly Smith lived in one of the cottages in the foreground and Ramsey School was situated opposite, it now being the War Memorial village hall.

Above: Wash Cottage, *c.*1914, situated at the far end of the village at Wash Corner where it joins Tinker Street. Wash Cottage, still inhabited today, was a cottage for farm workers from Hill House Farm. The gentleman standing alongside the cottage with his pony and cart is possibly George Cole.

Left: Sonny Gray with his dog at Hill House Farm, 1921.

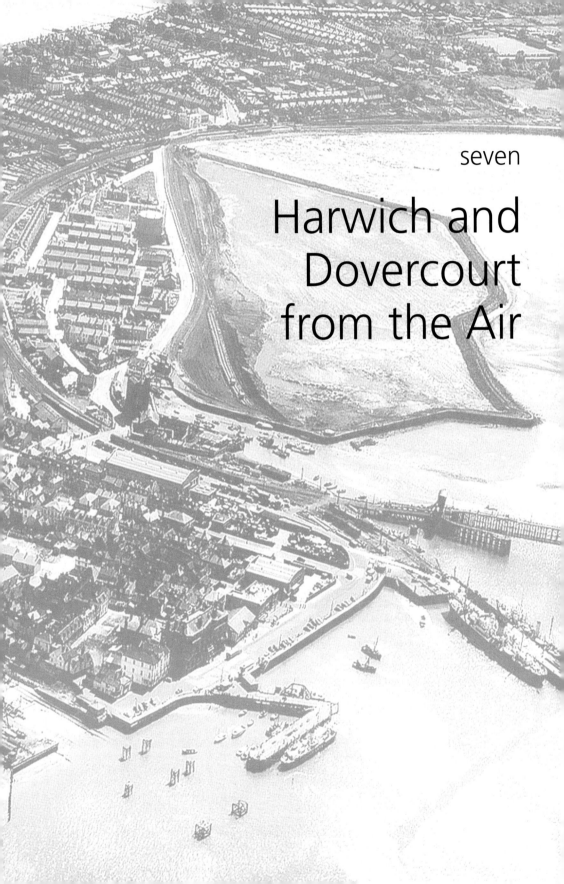

seven

Harwich and Dovercourt from the Air

Aerial photograph of recently extended facilities at Dovercourt, West End and beach, 1932. This view clearly shows the new road and promenade, along with the newly constructed boating lake, yachting pond, swimming pool and huge paddling pool. (Photograph by kind permission of Aerofilms Ltd. No.C1131)

Opposite above: A close-up shot of the West End bay, 1932. Butlins amusements are visible, as are the tennis courts of the new Sports Club. The borough surveyor, it would seem, had great difficulty in lining up the beach huts! (Photograph by kind permission of Aerofilms Ltd. No.39291)

Opposite below: Birds-eye view of Harwich Esplanade and town, 1932. An unspoilt scene of this area, showing centre left the Ordnance buildings, centre right the Three Cups Hotel with the original three floors and the tree-lined Wellington Road. (Photograph by kind permission of Aerofilms Ltd)

Above: Harwich Quay and old town, 1963, showing the first stages of the Navy Yard development and the newly erected Trinity House buildings. (Photograph by kind permission of Aerofilms Ltd)

Opposite above: Harwich old town, 1932, showing the new buildings of Harbour Crescent at the bottom of the picture and in the centre the open space that would become St Helen's Green housing development. (Photograph by kind permission of Aerofilms Ltd)

Opposite below: A 1959 view of Harwich and Dovercourt. The Bathside bay was still undeveloped and the shipyard still in use. (Photograph by kind permission of Aerofilms Ltd)

Angel Gate and Navyard Wharf, 1973. It's interesting to note that it was possible to walk under the buildings on the beach owned by Budworths and that the Harwich Harbour Board complex had not been built. (Photograph by kind permission of Aerofilms Ltd)

eight

Parkeston Quay

Hook Continental Boat Train, 1927, a new Harwich (Parkeston Quay) Continental express train from Liverpool Street to connect with the boats bound for the Continent. Consisting of eleven bogie coaches and two Pullman cars, the total weight with engine was 542 tons. This train was the pride of the Great Eastern Railway and was considered to be more than equal to the much-publicised *Flying Scotsman*. In 1930 the company commissioned Josiah Wedgwood to supply new dessert plates depicting six designs of principal Cathedrals. These plates would be used on the Harwich-Hook service and passengers could place an order to purchase them at the end of their journey.

Parkeston Quay, *c*.1928, showing the GER Turbine SS *Archangel* (formally *St Petersburg*) berthed alongside the Quay.

Right: Passengers disembarking from the SS *Vienna*, Parkeston Quay, 1931. The picture shows the new electric-powered five-ton cranes and a bull-nosed Morris car in the foreground.

Middle: Great Eastern Railway station and hotel complex at Parkeston Quay, *c.*1930.

Bottom: The dining room in the hotel on the Quay, *c.*1928, showing the plush fittings and lavish surroundings that the continental traveller might enjoy.

Construction of the new West End terminal, 1931. The railway company found that it was becoming more difficult to meet the ever-increasing demand on its facilities and decided to increase the capacity of the Quay. This photograph shows the early stages of its construction.

The finished West End extension, 1934. This development included a new station, Customs facilities, and three new, modern berths. The well-known Harwich Force Commander, Admiral Sir Reginald Tyrwhitt, officially opened the complex on 1 November 1934; the band of HM Royal Marines provided the music on this memorable occasion.

'Three new luxury ships' poster, 1929. LNER had ordered three new ships for the continental routes and commissioned the well-known marine artist F.H. Mason to design illustrations for a poster to mark the occasion of the introduction of the service. This poster is the result of his endeavours.

SS *Vienna* moored in the Stour at Parkeston Quay, 1929, in readiness for her maiden voyage to the Hook of Holland on 15 July 1929. She was the first of the three sister ships to join the fleet on the continental service. In 1932 the *Vienna* embarked on a number of weekend cruises and occasionally a mystery cruise would be offered, when passengers usually awoke to find themselves in the Channel Islands! In early 1936 the cruises proved so popular that LNER workshops at Parkeston Quay extended the aft boat deck to increase facilities.

Part of the cruising crew of the SS *Vienna*, 1933. The *Vienna* was advertised as the most luxurious cross-channel ferry afloat. She continued to carry on cruising until requisitioned by the Royal Navy in 1940 for use as a troopship, working mainly from Southampton to the French ports. After the war she reverted to the Harwich/Hook route, carrying up to 1,500 troops from the British Army of the Rhine. 1960 saw her last arrival at Parkeston, after which she was then towed to Belgium to be scrapped.

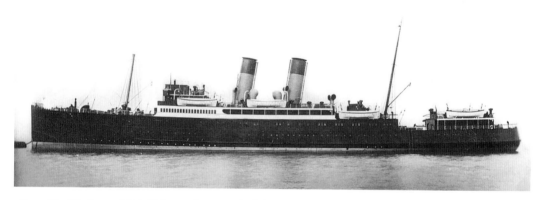

Above: The SS *Prague*, 1934. This was the second of the 'three ships' to arrive at Parkeston Quay. Built at John Brown's shipyard on the Clyde, the *Prague* had a service speed of 21 knots. She was delivered on 22 February 1930 and made her first trip to the Hook on 1 March.

Opposite below: SS *Prague* as a hospital ship in 1940, after being requisitioned by the Royal Navy as a hospital ship and trooper. The *Prague* made trips to Dunkirk and was returning with 3,000 French troops when she was hit by shore batteries and attacked by aircraft. She suffered considerable damage, and the troops were transferred to a nearby warship. The *Prague* was taking on water, so the vessel made its way to Deal and was run aground to save her. She resumed her tasks after repairs and made numerous trips to Normandy, bringing back the war-wounded. Whilst at Barrow for a refit a fire broke out, followed by an explosion, causing the ship to list and sink. She was written-off and finally scrapped.

Left, above: SS *Prague*'s first-class smoking room, *c.*1934, showing the ornate décor and the plush surroundings. The *Prague*, *Vienna* and *Amsterdam* were the first ships to be able to boast on-board shops.

Left: First-class entrance on the promenade deck of SS *Prague*, 1934. The trio of ships were all fitted and laid out in the same style.

SS *Amsterdam*, *c*.1930. Latest sister ship to join the Hook service, her maiden voyage occurred on 26 April 1930. Requisitioned by the Royal Navy in 1939, she was the last ship to leave Le Harvre before the enemy blew up the town. 1944 saw her rebuilt as a hospital ship and between 1944 and 1945 the *Amsterdam* made fifty-seven trips to Normandy, bringing back the war-wounded in dangerous conditions. On 7 August 1944 she was mined returning from Normandy and sank within fifteen minutes. Her master's main concern was for the badly wounded on board and it was due to his leadership that nearly all were saved in the short time before the ship sank.

Above: Una Road, Parkeston, *c*.1930. The shop on the corner belonged to E.K. Wright, and the road led to the brickworks of Edward Saunders. The picture shows how traffic-free the streets were at that time.

Opposite middle, left: C.T. Seago & Son fish merchants shop, Garland Road, Parkeston, *c*.1920. Mrs Seago is seen outside the shop with the family dog. The shop sold both fish and chips and wet fish. A close look at the sign-writing will reveal that the letters are painted in a fish design.

Opposite middle, right: Hugh Seago at the reins of his father's horse and cart on Dovercourt Green accompanied by Ken Day, 1936.

Opposite below: A view of Parkeston from the 'Bridges', *c*.1930. The open fields are long gone, and the large chimney, centre of picture, was that of Parkeston Quay's independent electric generating station, built in 1901.

Left: Edward Saunders brickworks, *c.*1928. The firm of Saunders were well-known builders in the area, employing 150 workers making bricks and tiles. A great number of houses were built using bricks from these works. A large kiln is shown on the right of the picture. The works have long since ceased production and are now subject to a controversial planning application for housing. Edward Street in the village is named after Mr Saunders.

Left: Bomb damage resulting from a Zeppelin raid at Tyler Street during the First World War.

Above: Empire day celebrations at Parkeston School, *c.*1920

Left: The ships' cleaning ladies pose at Hamilton Park, 1950s. From left to right, front row, are: Mrs Dean,-?-, -?-, Mrs Broom, Dot Webb, -?-, -?-. Middle row: R. Musk, Mrs Whitland, -?-, Mrs Day, -?-. Top: Rosie Preston, Mrs Thorpe. The other ladies are unknown.

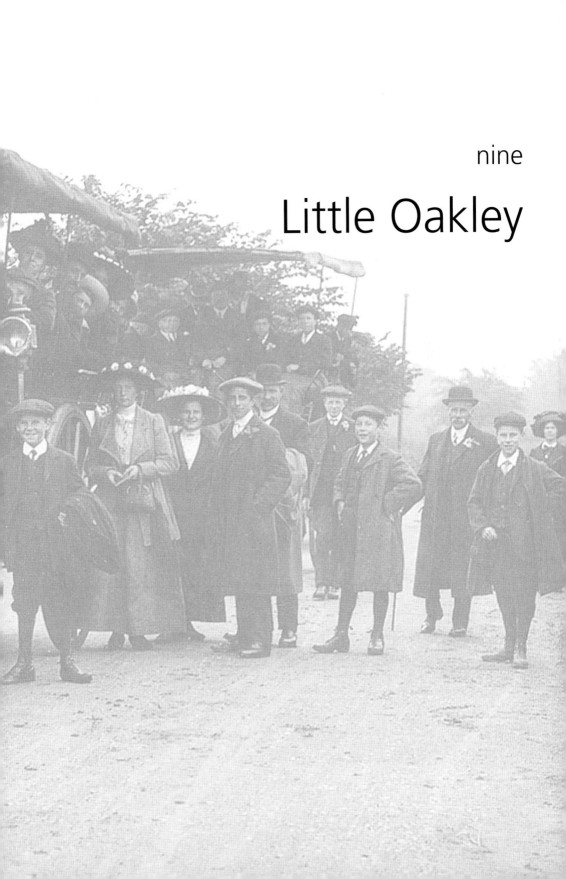

nine

Little Oakley

Above: Harwich Road, looking toward Cherry Tree corner, 1910. Mrs Peters is pushing the pram, and the butcher's cart from St Osyth is driven by Mr Wrycraft.

The Cherry Tree pub, *c.*1949. The Essex and Suffolk foxhounds gather to receive their stirrup-cup prior to taking to the fields in search of reynard.

Above: A gleaming new charabanc, loaded with regulars from the Cherry Tree pub in readiness for their annual outing to Clacton, July 1924.

Opposite top: Fulton Hall Dairy, *c.*1928. This image is typical of the modernisation of milk production and delivery. The horse and cart milk delivery had been exchanged for modern vans, and the cowmen and delivery drivers are wearing their new hygienic clothing. The milk was dispensed from sterile bottles instead of churns and the cows were machine milked.

Opposite middle: Mr Jack Smith and his son outside their home, *c.*1930. This home was a war surplus prefabricated building which served as troop accommodation at the army camp on Little Oakley marshes. After the war this wood and asbestos-constructed building was rebuilt in Mayes Lane, where it stood for many years.

Threshing contractors bag up the corn at Burnt House Farm during the summer of 1912.

Little Oakley Church of England School pupils, 1932. From left to right, back row: Basil Moore, Queenie Weaver, Eileen Nevard, Stella Ward, Joyce Peters, Connie Osborne, Lenna Wickham and John Barker. Middle row: Sybil Chote, Pat Ward, Myrtle Lord, Joyce Allen, Lily Mold, Kathleen Wallace, Babs Lord, -?-, Elsie Osborne, Laura Eagle. Front row: John Horslett, D. Chote, George Barker, Leonard Barrel, Ron Deex, William Oldroyd, Edward Oldroyd, Mervyn Hatcher, Fred Lord.

St Mary's Church, *c.*1948. Church records began in 1558. The church contained four bells housed in a stone tower and was built on isolated farmland with no housing nearby. Devoted parishioners had to traverse several fields to attend services. The church has been deconsecrated and is now a private residence.

Unveiling of the War Memorial in 1947 at St Mary's Church, with the Revd Redgrave giving the blessing. The choirboys to the left are Barry and Russell Thomas and John Humm. On the right, with their backs to the camera, are Mr and Mrs Barrell snr, and Mr Barrell jnr with his son Willie.

Circus elephants outside the Cherry Tree, 11 June 1945. The elephants were on their way to Harwich to perform, after travelling from Walton. The Little Oakley schoolchildren were given half a day off to attend the circus.

Little Oakley Chapel Sunday School outing, *c.*1920.

ten

Great Oakley

Sid May with his lorry laden with fruit and vegetables ready for his Dovercourt round, 1930. E.J. Keeble of Hall Farm employed Mr May for fifty-five years.

Explosive and Chemical Works munitions employees, 1914. This factory, built in 1901, produced ordnance for the military during both world wars. Because of the nature of this work the factory was a target for enemy aircraft.

Gt Oakley Main Street, 1905, showing the limited amount of shops. This small village did, however, boast four public houses. The Three Cups is in the foreground, right, and the Castle is a few doors away. It is claimed this pub was the last in Essex to stage a cockfight.

Four local lads sample the brew in the Maybush pub, 1960. Pictured, left to right, are Brian (Dooda) Deeks, Colin Wrycraft, Peter Oakley and Johnny (Chunky) Mowle.

Gt Oakley War Memorial and Main Street, *c*.1924. The War Memorial was unveiled on 31 January 1920 by Captain St John of the Royal Navy to commemorate the twenty-five village men who gave their lives during the First World War. The Memorial was erected on the spot where the first recruitment meeting was held at Gt Oakley during the Great War, when many local lads signed up to serve the King. Mrs Mann is standing by the telegraph pole and the Morris bull-nosed car owned by Mr Boardman is parked outside the Three Cups Hotel.

The street looking west towards School Corner, *c*.1920. On the right is the harness and saddlemakers of Richard Blowers. Then we see the old post office, The Swan public house and yard, and then the police house.

A snow scene of the street seen from the opposite direction, *c*.1918. The building on the right was a wheelwrights and carpenters shop run by Mr Cooper-Keeble. Mr Ernest Murrills owned the shop to the left.

This Wallis photograph captures the Offord family outside their home in 1913.

Above: Bus depot at Gt Oakley, owned by Dick Hooks, *c.*1940. Mr Hooks was a pioneer of private coach travel in the area.

Middle: The 'moat' at the west end of the street, *c.*1911. Behind the moat was a large house aptly named Moat Villa, long since demolished. The white gate on the left leads to Holt Farm.

Below: The High Street and windmill, *c.*1870. The mill was built in 1795 and was run in conjunction with a steam mill that was erected in 1835. Owing to the decline in the milling industry in the 1890s, the windmill ceased operations. Thereafter the mill fell into disrepair and it was eventually destroyed by fire in 1948.

eleven

Mistley

Mistley railway station, *c.*1906. The station was on the Harwich/Manningtree branch line and was built when the line was opened in 1854. In its heyday the station was awarded over thirty 'Best Kept Station' awards. In the background are the EDME malt extract works that have been on this site since the 1880s.

Mistley Quay, as seen from 'Coke Quay', *c.*1910. The Maltings of Free Rodwell can be seen in the centre of picture. Robert Free, William Rodwell, Robert E. Rodwell and E.N. Heneage formed the company in 1893, and in 1904 the factory was producing 100,000 quarters of brewer's malt per annum.

Mistley High Street, c.1914, with the Thorn Hotel on the left. The Swan Basin to the right was designed by the famous architect Robert Adams, and was to become part of George Rigby's ambitious scheme to make Mistley a Georgian port and Spa town. Unfortunately the project did not materialise due to lack of funds.

Mistley Place, c.1950. Built in 1821 for Edward Norman, the building was later to become a school. In its latter days Brooks Mistley took over the premises for use as a sports club for its employees. Brooks, who had their own quays at Mistley, were famous for their agricultural products and they also had a prize-winning cattle and dairy herd. The building itself has since been demolished.

Brooks main garage, *c.*1950, showing some of the fleet of over eighty vehicles that delivered agricultural products including grain, seeds and cattle feed. The Brooks family had run the firm since 1863.

The lorry repair workshop, *c.*1950. All the firm's vehicles were serviced and repaired on site by their own skilled engineers, which ensured the efficient running of the fleet to meet maximum capacity.

The busy accounts department of Brooks Mistley, *c*.1950.

A convoy of Brooks' lorries at Parkeston Quay, *c*.1950. This was a consignment of red clover seed destined for Canada; this particular load was the largest ever to be shipped by the company as an individual lot.

The seed laboratory, Brooks Mistley, c.1950. All seeds were tested and approved for high quality before despatch.

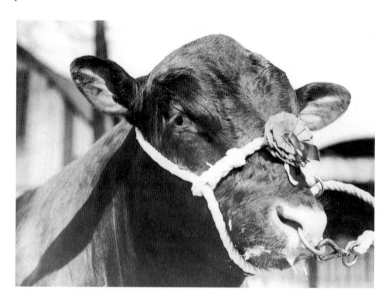

'Mistley Amorist', Brooks' head of stock bull, c.1950. Born at Mistley on 8 March 1939, he won first prize at the Red Poll Cattle Society show and, when two years old, was sold to HM King George VI for his Red Poll herd at Sandringham. He was used for seven years and during that time sired many notable animals including Royal Frolic, which won the Championship at the Royal Agricultural Show.

twelve

Armed Forces

The Suffolk 'Button Boys' Training Regiment, 1916. This group photograph was taken at the Royal Oak football field. The regiment was named 'button boys' because at the outbreak of war, Lord Kitchener asked for 100,000 volunteers to join the armed forces. He actually got over one million, which put a strain on the ordnance department, who did not have enough cap badges to go round. Therefore regimental buttons, which had insignia on them, were put onto the soldiers' caps as a short-term measure. The proper badges are worn by officers and NCOs except for the sergeant major, who is badged as the Essex Regiment. Amongst those pictured is at least one Lewis gunner and two officers with wound stripes. Others are wearing good conduct stripes and marksman badges. The regiment would have been tented at Barrack field, with some training taking place at the Redoubt.

Dovercourt station during the First World War, *c*.1916. Army carthorses were used to shunt the supply trucks into the sidings enabling them to be off-loaded onto to the waiting lorries that would re-supply the Harwich Garrison.

Overleaf: Early 'mast manning' ceremony at HMS *Ganges*, Shotley, *c*.1908. Just across the river from Harwich the HMS *Ganges* boys' training school was built. In 1889 the training ship *Ganges* arrived at Harwich from her previous berth at Falmouth. The locals gave the *Ganges* boys a warm welcome; the lads would come ashore and entertain the citizens with hornpipes, musical dumbbells, singing and recitation. In 1903 the Admiralty decided that a new shore establishment should be built at either Harwich or Shotley, and much to the dismay of the Borough of Harwich, Shotley was the chosen site. However Shotley barracks continued to associate with Harwich rather than Ipswich, and was supplied from Harwich and also used the town's postal address. *Ganges*' shore establishment had no mast of their own, but in 1907 they acquired the foremast of HMS *Cordelia*, a frigate paid off in 1900. The mast was towed from Sheerness by sea and when it arrived at Shotley Pier the boys manhandled the 143ft mast up the steep hill; the operation took over five hours. The mast was rigged and the boys would be made to 'man the mast'. The barracks are no longer used but the mast lives on and has a preservation order attached to it, so its future is safeguarded.

Voluntary services, June 1939. This photograph was taken in the Regal cinema car park as part of a recruiting campaign for the Territorial Army, ARP, Auxiliary Fire Service and other voluntary organisations. The film *The Warning* was screened at the cinema in conjunction with the parade, aimed at drawing public attention to the dangers posed by air raids. The campaign was called 'How you can serve your Country'.

Beacon Hill battery, 1936. This 6-inch gun was manned by members of the local Territorial Army. Percy Cardy and Ike Hart are to the left of the gun's breach.

Suffolk Regiment working party at the rear of High House Farm, Tollgate, *c.*1916.

Engineers at Warner's Holiday Camp, *c.*1940. The War Office had taken over the holiday camp and it was used first as a camp for soldiers passing from England to Germany, called Headquarters No.4 centre. Later the Royal Engineers erected perimeter fencing and made the grounds secure so that it could be used as a prisoner of war camp. Photographed are the engineers from the Harwich Garrison erecting the high fences.

War veterans meet up outside All Saints Church School after the unveiling of the Upper Dovercourt War Memorial, c.1920.

Royal Navy Harwich defences, c.1941. An unusual sight of a mobile Oerlikon ack–ack gun mounted on a lorry manned by sailors of the Royal Navy.

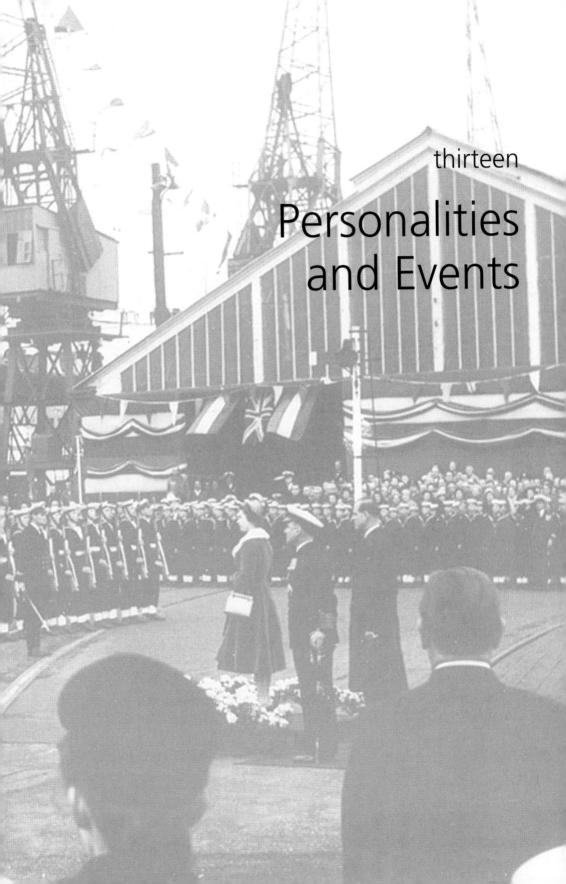

thirteen

Personalities and Events

Parkeston Hamilton Park, early 1920s. Parkeston celebrates May Day and the local orchestra entertains the crowds; Frances Storr is playing the piano.

May Day sword dance performed by the older Parkeston village children, c.1924.

Junior Busybodies, *c*.1922. These talented youngsters used to entertain regularly at Cliff Hall and several other local venues. Doris Toft is in the front row holding the violin, and her father was the leader of the well-known travelling entertainers. 'The Tofts', who played at most of the large seaside resorts, must have encouraged these children to follow in their footsteps.

The local branch of the St Dunstan's Carol League, 1922. This group was made up of all denominations who were collecting for the St Dunstan's blinded soldiers fund. They would start off at Harwich and travel via Church Street, Main Road and Fronks Road, and carry out performances along the way. The carollers wore mortarboards and distinctive red masks and capes.

The Rips Concert Party in Cliff Park, *c.*1923. The Rips were popular local entertainers. Amongst those pictured are Christopher Pennick and Gladys Gooch.

Capt Fryatt's funeral procession leaves Dovercourt station for its journey to Upper Dovercourt Church for the burial service and internment.

An unknown funeral procession goes past the top of Manor Road, *c.*1916. The vast crowds and the high military presence would seem to indicate this was the funeral of a very high-ranking officer.

Uncaptioned photograph of a parade on Upper Dovercourt Green outside the cemetery, *c.*1915

HMS *Blenheim* outing, July 1922. The *Blenheim*, launched on 26 May 1908, was a Blake Class Cruiser stationed at Harwich as a depot ship. Here we see the engine-room artificers and their families ready to board one of Starling's charas.

Above: Harwich Guides with the Scroll of Friendship, July 1950. Between 21 and 31 July, Scrolls of Friendship (messages) were passed hand-to-hand from the furthermost parts of the UK until they reached Oxford. At a monster camp HRH Princess Margaret presented them to twenty-seven leaders of national delegations as a message of welcome and friendship. Some of the guides playing their part in the Harwich area are pictured here with their bicycles. Left to right are Joyce Gooding, Rosemary Double and Wendy Wrycraft.

Right: The Duchess of Kent steps ashore to visit HMS *Badger* in 1941. The Duchess visited this shore establishment as well as the wren's quarters in Cliff Road and the Elco on the seafront. Wren officer Snow is on the quayside.

Opposite below: The local school is the venue for the 1st Parkeston Girl Guides to be photographed.

Left: Joseph Edward Gant 1863–1927, hurdlemaker, who had his premises at Upper Dovercourt next to Pound Farm.

Below: Parkeston guy carnival group revived the carnival that the shipwrights used to organise until the Second World War. A rare photograph from 1954 shows these Parkeston youngsters dressed up for the first carnival since the war. A few years later the venue was moved back to Harwich and the carnival still carries on today.

Right: Ike Hart, born 1840. Well-known local fisherman and character, when he wasn't fishing he found time to have thirteen children!

Below: Arthur Barnard and Charlie ? at the West End beach, mid-1950s. They were the West End deckchair attendants and Arthur was also in charge of the unusual jockey-weighing scales.

Left: Len (Goosey) Gosling DSM, demonstrating his rope-working skills, *c.*1970. Len had many talents – his seafaring background was a great advantage when it came to making any number of intricate rope items and superb corn dollies were one of his specialities. A keen supporter of the Harwich guy carnival and the hospital fêtes, he constructed several fairground-type attractions for these occasions. Len died in 1987 and is sadly missed.

Below: Jack Howlett at the summer carnival, 1964. Jack was the local turf accountant, and would always take advantage of any opportunity to dress up and raise funds for charity. He is seen with a very smart Palomino horse, all set to join the procession.

One of the many local bands, *c.*1946. This picture was taken at a dance at the Phoenix Hotel and features, on trumpet, Wally Smith; on saxophone, Jim Simpson; and on drums, Bill Calver.

MV *Frederica*/Radio Caroline, *c.*1965. Ronan O'Rahilly created Britain's first commercial radio station when he fitted out the 700-ton ex-ferry the *Frederica*. The vessel appeared, moored off Harwich, on Good Friday 1964 and she made her first broadcast on Easter Saturday playing the Beatles record *Can't Buy Me Love*. Harwich played an important role in Radio Caroline's life when local fishing boats would re-supply her under cover of darkness and with strict secrecy, after the government forbade dealings with the radio station. Among the DJs who came ashore on crew-change days were Simon Dee, Keith Scues and Dave Lee Travis.

Royal Yacht *Britannia* at Parkeston Quay, March 1958. HRH Queen Elizabeth takes the salute from the Royal Navy guard of honour with HRH Duke of Edinburgh standing behind. The Royal party had come from Harwich Town Hall where they had met with local dignitaries before travelling to Parkeston to board *Britannia* for a state visit to Holland.

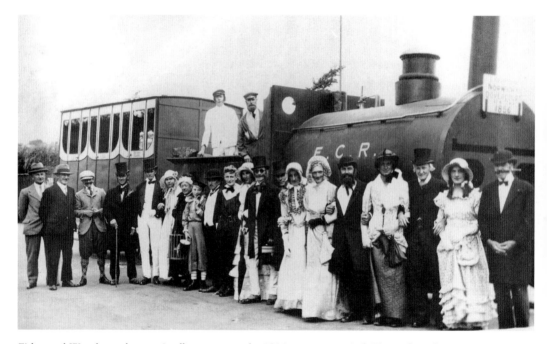

Fisher and Woods mock-up train all set to enter the 1934 summer carnival. Pictured on the engine are, left, E. Osborn, and right, L. Westlake. The others, left to right, are: Nelson Woods, Oliver Fisher, A. Bowman, W. Rowland, F. Goodwin, A. Ryder Utting, G. Shrive, F. Warren, C. Futter, N. Zeed, F. Rowland, H. Smith, W. Harvey, E. Wright, H. Seaborn, -?-, L. Barfield, J. Tagg, E. Closs.

fourteen

Sport

Harwich County Youth Centre football first and second teams, *c.*1949, North East Essex champions. Left team, from left, back row: Cyril Moles, Mayhew, M. Rose, R. Manhood, ? Smith, ? Betts, B. Smith. Front row: ? Bowgen, D. Bacon, Bill Harvey, P. Bowling, Jack Barker. Right team, from right, back row: ? Chapman, –?–, M. Raynor, ? Green, John Dean, ? Elwood, Ken Roberts. Front row: Ray Brundle, Terry Bacon, Gordon Whiffing, Ken Brundle, Wilf Rose, ? Shepherd, ? Hudson.

Dovercourt Wednesday cricket team, 1930s. Back row: ? Cook, –?–, Alf Bury, –?–, Charlie Cooper-Keeble, –?–, –?–, –?–. Front row: ? Hall, –?–, –?–, –?–, Stan Robinson.

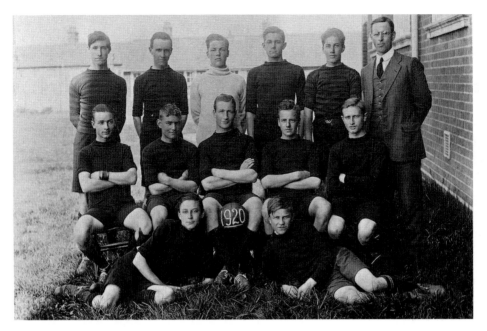

Harwich County High School first eleven football team, 1920. From left to right, back row: Springall, Smith, Wrigley, Flinders, Clarke (reserve), Milk. Middle row: White, Beaney, Mann, (captain), Silburn, Jessup. Front row: Cann and Last.

Moto-ball match on the Yeast Factory sports field, 1964. The Harwich team attack their opponent's goal. Pictured, left to right, are: –?–, Tony Macey, ? Mowley, Dick Dale. Moto-ball was played with a 15-inch leather ball and five players per side. At one time there were ten teams playing in the British league. Harwich joined the European league and played France, Holland and Germany. They also travelled overland to Russia to play in the World Championships. The sport of moto-ball has lost its popularity over recent years.

Right: Harwich motorcycle club man Phil Burley passengers a racing sidecar outfit driven by Mick Potter in the 1971 Isle of Man TT. The outfit was powered by a BSA 750cc 3-cylinder engine. They finished in eighth position, averaging a speed of 80.18mph, and gained a silver Replica.

Middle: Harwich and Parkeston FC with their trophies in 1921.

Harwich Rangers football team, *c.*1947. From left to right, back row: Bob Tye, Tucker Tye, Bill Chambers, Jos Parker, Albert Tuffin, Bill Hammond, Nat (Royal) Wringe, Buck Ryan, Fred Parker, Arthur Orton, Harry Harman, Dennis O'Dea. Front row: 'Col' Baker, Danny Sorrel, Johnny Pells, Billy Bennet, Harold Good.

fifteen

Dovercourt Bay

The 'giddy shrimp' at Dovercourt, 1920. The shrimp has long associations with Harwich and Dovercourt mainly because Harwich had a large fleet of shrimp boats in the early 1900s, and the town became well known for its quality shrimps. This postcard has twelve photographs on a strip inside and was a novelty souvenir.

Crowds pack the promenade and seafront slopes to watch the 1912 regatta. The Cliff Hotel is in the background.

Above: Road-widening of Main Road, top of Bobbits Hill, *c.*1926. This road-widening scheme was funded in part by the government with the aim of reducing unemployment in the area; the Royal Oak pub is on the right and Harwich and Parkeston football ground on the left.

Right: Jack Beales Amusement Arcade, High Street, 1951. This arcade opened amongst controversy after the war, but nevertheless it proved very popular with the young. It is remembered how parents would ban their children from frequenting the arcade which, of course, made it a more exciting place to visit.

BEALES'S
AMUSEMENT ARCADE
"Dovercourt's brightest spot"

Open Daily 10 a.m. - 10 p.m.
For your Entertainment

125 HIGH STREET DOVERCOURT
Opposite Railway Station

Construction of new houses, Fronks Road, *c.*1913. These houses were sited on the north side of Fronks Road at its junction with Highfield Avenue. The water tower can be seen in the distance and no more houses appear to have been built between Highfield Avenue and Manor Lane.

The Hill School dressed overall and floodlit to mark the jubilee of King George V and Queen Mary in 1935.

Above left: Waitresses from The Retreat, *c.*1920. This building had a large indoor skating rink and could provide catering facilities for 2,000. Dr Barnardo children would often holiday here and one of the waitresses can recall filling mattresses with straw for the children to sleep on.

Above right: W. Dunn, grocer and fruiterer, Lee Road, 1935. This picturesque little shop was popular with the residents of the area.

Dovercourt children congregate to pose for a photograph in Hordle Street, *c.*1916. The large wisteria on the corner house wall must have been a magnificent sight when in bloom.

Smith's fruiterers shop, c.1890. This was one of the first purpose-built shops in the High Street, and is situated at the junction with what is known now as Kingsway. The shop appears to be isolated, as major development in the area was yet to take place. Standing in the doorway are, left, Mrs Smith, and right, Mrs Nellie Hustler.

Acknowledgements

Very special thanks to my family for their support with this project, and to Peter Goodwin for his help and enthusiasm. I would also like to acknowledge the assistance of the following: Kathleen McCafferey, Brian Smith, Betty Crawley, Dave Tricker, Dennis Neal, Don Lungley, Ruth Spendly, Linda Stephens, Ike Hart, Bette Calver, Les Double, Barbara Sansom, Paul Beck, Dick Smith, Cath Simpson, Terry Smith, Stan Beacham, British AeroFilms and all the other people who were kind enough to loan me photographs or provided me with useful information.